DISCOVER
The Lake District

Val Corbett

▲ **Beatrix Potter** Hill Top at Near Sawrey, the picturesque farmhouse close to Hawkshead where Beatrix Potter wrote and illustrated many of her popular animal stories. The house was recreated for the film *Miss Potter*. When Beatrix died in 1943 she left Hill Top to the National Trust, with the stipulation that it be left exactly as it was for future visitors to enjoy.

CONTENTS

MYRIAD

Windermere

Many visitors catch their first view of the Lake District as they drive over the crest of the hill from Kendal. The breathtaking Windermere is the first lake they encounter. At its northern end is the historic town of Ambleside; packed with pubs and restaurants, this is an ideal base from which to explore the area. A few miles north of Windermere are Rydal and Grasmere where the poet William Wordsworth lived with his family. Just to the west lies the charming, higgledy-piggledy village of Hawkshead and, close by, Hill Top, the home of Beatrix Potter.

▲ Bowness The car ferry to Far Sawrey crosses the lake just south of Bowness – a fun way to visit Beatrix Potter's home at Far Sawrey. Operating all year round, this is the only Lake District ferry to carry cars.

▼ Historic ferries Windermere bustles with the comings and goings of small boats and pleasurecraft, including the *Osprey*. Built in 1902, it is just one of the many splendid wooden boats that ply the lake. The Steamboat Museum at Windermere has a superb collection of these historic craft.

AMBLESIDE

▲▼ Ambleside St Mary's church spire dominates the pretty town of Ambleside. As a young man Wordsworth was distributor of stamps for Westmorland and he had his office in the town. A stained-glass window and memorial chapel in the church commemorates the life of the poet, his wife Mary and sister Dorothy. Ambleside is a lively town and every August hosts the Lake District Summer Music Festival.

◀ Waterhead Steamers and launches sail all year round to Bowness and Lakeside from the ferry terminal at Waterhead. For the intrepid, a pleasant way to explore the lake is to hire a rowing boat from the landing stage.

▼▶ Stock Bridge The oldest part of the town is clustered around Peggy Hill, a steep climb from Stock Bridge. In the past, Stock Beck powered many of the local mills.

RYDAL

▶ **Rydal Hall** This grand 17th-century house was once the home of the le Fleming family, the Wordsworths' landlords. Now a conference and retreat centre, the formal gardens are open to the public; one of the highlights is a series of waterfalls which plunge down a rocky ravine. The oldest viewing house in the country, which dates from 1669, is situated below the lower waterfall. ▼

▲ **Rydal Mount** Home to the Wordsworths from 1813 to 1850, this beautiful Lakeland villa has a lived-in atmosphere which has changed little since Wordsworth's day. The house, which is open to the public, contains portraits, personal possessions and first editions.

From the summerhouse there is a dramatic view over nearby Rydal Water. Dora's Field, between the house and the main road, was planted with hundreds of daffodils as a memorial to the poet's daughter who died in 1847; Wordsworth died in 1850.

▼ Rydal Water One of the Lake District's smallest lakes, Rydal Water lies in a sheltered bowl and early morning mists are common. A popular walk hugs the western shore of the lake, before crossing the river Rothay leading to a high-level path that drops into Rydal village.

▲ **Grasmere** At the very heart of the Lake District, Grasmere was Wordsworth's home for the most creative period of his life. He lived at Dove Cottage from 1799-1808 and it was here that he entertained a vast circle of friends including Samuel Taylor Coleridge. Looking across Grasmere (above) the white face of the Prince of Wales hotel is visible on the far side; Dove Cottage is tucked just behind to the right. The view shows Helm Crag to the left, the Pass of Dunmail Raise and the soaring slopes of Seat Sandal.

▲ **Church of St Oswald**
William, Dorothy and Mary Wordsworth are buried in the church of St Oswald in Grasmere. Their gravestone is a place of pilgrimage for lovers of the Lakeland poets.

▶ **The Langdales** Just south-west of Grasmere lie the two Langdale valleys. Great Langdale (right), is dominated by the Pikes – Pike O'Stickle and Harrison Stickle on the right, while further right is Pavey Arc. For an exhilarating drive, head for the Wrynose Pass. One of the steepest roads in England it sweeps past Hardknott Fort, the site of a Roman camp and onto Eskdale and the coast of West Cumbria.

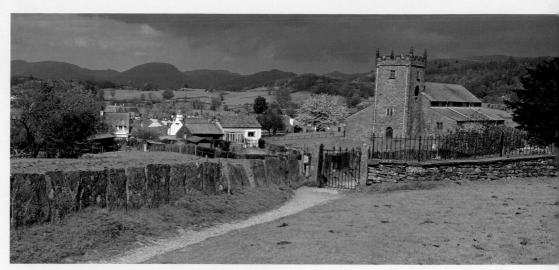

▲ **Hawkshead** Between Windermere
and the northern end of Coniston Water,
Hawkshead is a compact maze of white-
washed buildings dominated by the
church of St Michael's and All Angels.
William Wordsworth and his brother
John were both pupils at the old grammar
school, which is now a museum. The
town houses the Beatrix Potter gallery,
a 17th-century building which was once
the office of local solicitor William Heelis
who married the author in 1913.

◄ **Blea Tarn** Sited between Great and
Little Langdale, Blea Tarn is one of the
most accessible of the upland lakes. This
wintry scene shows the Langdale Pikes
with Pike O'Stickle on the left and
Harrison Stickle on the right.

Coniston

The pretty village of Coniston lies to the north-west of Coniston Water. It is the gateway to the Duddon estuary and the south Cumbrian coast. There have been copper mines in the area since Roman times and the fell behind the town, the Old Man of Coniston, is scarred with evidence of these activities. The area is rich in history – Brantwood was the lakeshore home of John Ruskin, the art critic and social reformer and, more recently, Donald Campbell perished on the lake in an attempt to break the world waterspeed record.

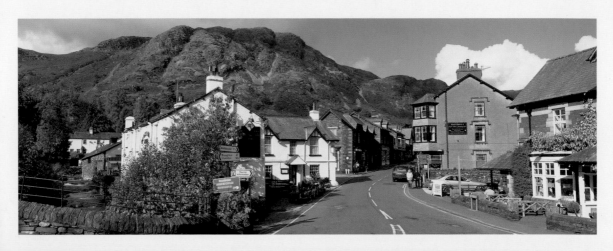

▲ **Coniston Old Man** This view looks across from the east bank of the lake to the town of Coniston with the Old Man of Coniston behind. In the foreground is High Bank Ground Farm, the setting for Arthur Ransome's famous children's novel *Swallows and Amazons*.

▼ **Coniston Water** On a still September morning the peaks of the Old Man and, to its right, Wetherlam tower above Coniston. This view is from Brantwood, the home of John Ruskin. It was considered by him to be the finest panorama in the Lake District.

SOUTHERN LAKELAND

▲ **Kelly Hall Tarn** This quiet lake lies only a short distance from the road running up the west side of Coniston Water. In the background are some of the Coniston fells, including Dow Crag and the Old Man.

▼ **Steam yacht** The restored steam yacht *Gondola* plies Coniston Water and calls at Brantwood.
The boat combines the workmanship of a Venetian gondola with that of a Victorian steamship.

▶ **Broughton-in-Furness** Seven miles from Coniston Water, Broughton is one of the Lakes' most attractive villages. Broughton Mills, just to the north, is set in an idyllic valley; Holy Innocents church is well worth a visit.

▼ Cartmel The priory church of St Mary and St Michael is reputed to be the most beautiful church in the north-west of England. It was founded in 1188 and towers over the town of Cartmel which sits on a small peninsula jutting into the flat expanse of Morecambe Bay.

▼▼ Duddon Estuary With a shoreline of 28 miles the Duddon estuary opens into the Irish Sea just north of Barrow-in-Furness. The estuary offers views of mountains, pale sand and sky that could almost be Hebridean. The highest mountain in the photograph is Black Combe which is detached from the main Lake District mountains; in the far distance to the right are the Coniston Fells.

Ullswater

Located between Pooley Bridge in the north and Glenridding in the south, Ullswater is regarded by many as the most beautiful of all the Lakes. The second largest in the region, the lake has two bends which divide it into three distinct stretches of water. The surrounding high fells contain some of Lakeland's best-known scenery: the steep-sided Striding Edge, Patterdale, Kirkstone Pass (Lakeland's highest mountain pass) and the Roman road on High Street. The Pooley Bridge boathouse is one of the most photographed locations in the Lake District.

▲ **Patterdale** On the road between the Kirkstone Pass and Ullswater, the Patterdale valley is a magnet for walkers and climbers. Towering above the small village is the Helvellyn range. The coast-to-coast long-distance footpath passes through the village.

◀ **Glencoyne Farm**
The view from the path to the cottages at Seldom Seen in Glencoynedale was one of Queen Victoria's favourites; it remains little changed since her day. The daffodils along the Glencoyne shoreline of Ullswater inspired a diary entry by Dorothy Wordsworth, part of which William included in his poem *I wandered lonely as a cloud*. Widely known as *Daffodils*, it is probably the most famous poem in the language.

15

▲ **Striding Edge** The route up to Helvellyn is one of the most popular walks in the Lake District. The summit is grassy and remarkably flat, but on its eastern side lies the knife-sharp ridge of Striding Edge. The narrow path falls away steeply on either side and can be dangerous, particularly in bad weather.

▼ **Hartsop** This unspoilt village is situated in a sheltered side valley near Brothers Water at the foot of the Kirkstone Pass. In the past the area was busy with mining; a short walk along the track to the Hayeswater reservoir leads to the ruins of the watercourse and wheel pit of the former Mires Head leadmine.

▲ **Angle Tarn** Lying high above Patterdale and Hartsop, Angle Tarn has a gentler appearance than many of the high tarns as it is cupped by surrounding crags and is unusually indented and reedy. A short climb opens up fine views to the west; in the far distance are the more northerly stretches of the Helvellyn range. The route of the coast-to-coast walk passes the tarn.

▶ **Haweswater**
A reservoir rather than a lake, Haweswater was created in the 1930s to provide water for Manchester. Its peaceful air belies the fact that submerged beneath the waters lies the old village of Mardale, drowned when the valley was flooded.

▲ Lowther Castle Situated five miles south of Penrith in beautiful parkland lies the spectacular ruin of Lowther Castle. Built in 1810, the castle fell into disrepair because of the notorious extravagance of the 5th Lord Lonsdale.

▼ Pooley Bridge This bustling village lies close to the northern tip of Ullswater. The Ullswater Steamer Company runs boats from the landings to Howtown and Glenridding which connect with excellent walks on the eastern side of the lake.

Derwent Water

Located on beautiful Derwent Water, with its stunning scenery and boating attractions, Keswick is the largest town in the Lake District. The surrounding area is packed with scenic attractions: Bassenthwaite and the three adjoining lakes of Buttermere, Crummock Water and Loweswater are all surrounded by lofty fells with a scattering of pretty villages. Literary and historic associations abound, particularly in Borrowdale and Buttermere. Close to Keswick is the dramatic Castlerigg Stone Circle, one of the most important prehistoric sites in Britain.

▲ **The town** Keswick's best-known landmark is the Moot Hall, which dates from 1813. It houses the tourist information centre and, at its west end, is the famous "one-handed" clock. In the past the hall served as a court-house, a museum, a prison and a local market.

▼ **Pleasure trips** From the boat landings it is possible to hire a rowing boat or take one of the many pleasure trips around the lake. There are splendid views of Cat Bells, Skiddaw and the five islands that grace Derwent Water including St Herbert's Island and Lord's Island, both of which are owned by the National Trust. The lake is surrounded by Borrowdale, Newlands and Skiddaw.

AROUND KESWICK

▲ **Derwent Water** The first snows of winter coat the summit of Skiddaw, in the distance across the lake. To the right the Ashness launch landing stage is one of seven around the lake. The traditional teak launches operate a frequent service throughout the year. The 12-mile circuit of the lake is too long for many walkers, but making use of the launches offers a variety of excellent shorter walks between stages.

▶ **Ashness Bridge** Taken on a chilly February morning, this view of the pack-horse bridge on the road to Watendlath is one of the Lake District's most treasured views. Derwent Water is visible in the far distance and, rising behind it, is the Skiddaw massif, partially topped with snow.

▼ **Castlerigg Stone Circle** Dating from around 3000BC, this impressive stone circle sits in a natural amphitheatre of fells to the east of Keswick. It is thought that the circle was originally made up of 70 stones. Today there are 38 forming a rough oval, within which there is an unusual small rectangular setting of another 10 stones. When snow is on the ground the circle takes on an almost other-worldly air and the surrounding mountains of Skiddaw, Blencathra and Lonscale Fell seem to crowd in around the site.

▲ **St Kentigern**
The parish church of St Kentigern is at Crosthwaite on the western edge of Keswick. Canon Rawnsley, the co-founder of the National Trust, was the vicar for 34 years. He is buried here, lying close to much of the countryside he helped to preserve.

◄ **Cat Bells**
The view across Derwent Water towards Keswick from the summit of Cat Bells shows Skiddaw and Blencathra behind the town.

21

BORROWDALE

▲ **Borrowdale** Stretching from the head of Derwent Water south to Seathwaite, Borrowdale is walled in by steep crags on all sides. The low-slung twin arches of Grange Bridge span the two branches of the river Derwent.

▼▶ **Seatoller** The tiny linked villages of Seatoller and Stonethwaite lie close to each other in Borrowdale. Seatoller is little more than a cluster of houses around a farm; the Yew Tree coffee house is an ideal stop for visitors.

▲▼ **Watendlath** Situated at the end of a narrow and twisting road leading from Derwent Water, the little hamlet of Watendlath, owned by the National Trust, is the kind of place where ducks and geese seem to have as equal a right to the road as cars. Watendlath Tarn is a great attraction for sightseers, otherwise the hamlet principally consists of a farmhouse or two, one selling teas and the other hiring rowing boats for trout-fishing. An ancient packhorse bridge crosses Watendlath Beck soon after it leaves the tarn. There is a National Trust tearoom at Caffle House in the village.

BUTTERMERE

◀▲▶ Buttermere One of three intercon-
nected lakes, this remote hamlet can be
reached either from the Newlands or
Honister Pass. The village is located close to
low-lying water meadows where cows were
kept, giving Buttermere its name. The view
above is from the opposite,
eastern end of the lake close to Gatesgarth
Farm. The village consists of little more
than a farm and two hotels, the Bridge and
the Fish. The latter became famous as the
home of Mary Robinson, "the beauty of
Buttermere", whose story is retold in the
book *The Maid of Buttermere* by Melvyn
Bragg. At the top of the lake near
Gatesgarth and at the foot of Fleetwith
Pike are the famous Buttermere pines.

◀ Crummock Water

This glorious view is from the southern end of Crummock Water and shows the forbidding slopes of Melbreak which run the full length of the lake on its western shoreline. Owned by the National Trust, Crummock Water is a quiet and peaceful spot. Small boats are permitted on the lake but they must be carried to the shore by hand. On the right – ablaze with the glow of dead bracken – are the slopes of the Rannerdale Knotts which, in contrast to their giant neighbours, offer a gentler climb to an attractive summit ridge. The little valley of Rannerdale is well-known for the bluebells which carpet its slopes in May and early June.

BASSENTHWAITE & THE NORTH

▲ **Bassenthwaite** Rich evening light illuminates the slopes of Skiddaw sweeping down to the waters of the lake. The peaceful, reedy east shore has an abundance of birdlife and, in summer, is blessed with great drifts of wildflowers. The little lakeside church of St Bega is worth a visit as is the unusual bee garden at historic Mirehouse.

▶ **Braithwaite** Nestling at the foot of Whinlatter Pass, with Bassenthwaite Lake a short distance away, this picturesque village is an ideal base for exploring the north-western lakes. Alfred Wainwright, author of the famous guidebooks, regarded this area, with its mix of fells and pastoral landscape, as the best of Lakeland.

▲ **Wythop Mill** The charming hamlet of Wythop Mill, originally the site of a large cornmill, is located off the road to Cockermouth. The village sits at the edge of the wide Wythop valley, with the northern slopes of Ling Fell as a backdrop.

Caldbeck This attractive village was the home of the Cumbrian huntsman John Peel; his ornate gravestone, in the churchyard of St Kentigern, draws many visitors. Hunting dominated his life and led to the famous song which commemorates his exploits.

Hesket Newmarket Lying close to Caldbeck, its larger neighbour, this pretty hamlet has a wide village green with houses on both sides. In the Old Crown Inn there is a logbook recording details of the "Old Crown Round", in which walkers must reach four local summits inside 20 hours.

Wasdale & the West

The western Lake District is one of the most remote regions of England – even the villages of this region, such as Boot and Wasdale Head seem like tiny islands in a sea of wild and untamed countryside. It is this very remoteness which attracts visitors to the area. The region contains Scafell Pike, England's highest mountain, and Wastwater, its deepest lake. To the north is the equally remote valley of Ennerdale. Head towards the coast and the scenery changes completely, especially around picturesque and historic towns such as St Bees and Ravenglass.

▲ **Wast Water** This is the first view of Wast Water most visitors see as they approach from the west. On the right are the rounded slopes of Scafell with Scafell Pike behind. Directly ahead is Great Gable whose perfect shape is used as the logo of the Lake District National Park. The inset photograph (below) shows the packhorse bridge which lies behind the Wasdale Head Inn at the far end of the lake.

◀ **Westmorland Cairn** This view of Wasdale from Great Gable is taken from a vantage point close to the Westmorland Cairn. It was built in 1876 by two brothers from Westmorland to mark what they regarded as the finest mountain viewpoint in the Lake District.

ESKDALE & WASDALE

▲ **Eskdale** This view of Eskdale, the remote valley which links central Lakeland with the west, shows Brotherilkeld Farm and the upper Eskdale valley from the slopes of Harter Fell. Some of the giants of the Lake District peaks can be seen at the end of the valley – Scafell, Scafell Pike, Esk Pike, Bowfell and Crinkle Craggs.

▼ **Wasdale Head** This tiny hamlet at the far end of Wasdale is situated in an arena of dramatic mountains. The Wasdale Show in early October takes place in a field next to the tiny St Olaf's church. This agricultural show features Herdwick sheep and a variety of traditional Cumbrian sporting events take place.

▲ **Nether Wasdale** The tiny settlement of Nether Wasdale is situated between Gosforth, Santon Bridge and Wast Water. From the wide village green of this pretty hamlet there are superb views of the Wasdale Screes which form a dramatic mile-long wall on the south side of the lake.

▼ **Ravenglass** The only coastal village within the National Park, Ravenglass was originally a Roman supply port at the western end of the route linking Hardknott Fort, High Street and Ambleside. The village is the terminal for the Ravenglass and Eskdale railway which runs for seven miles to Dalegarth in Eskdale.

ST BEES & ENNERDALE

▲▶ **St Bees** Four miles south of Whitehaven, this little town with its beautiful priory church, long sandy beach and fine sandstone headland contrasts with the rugged, mountainous scenery inland. The priory was established by Bega, an Irish nun who was ship-wrecked here in the 9th century. The 190-mile long coast-to-coast walk starts at St Bees Head and ends at Robin Hood's Bay in Yorkshire.

▼ **Muncaster Castle** Inland from Ravenglass lies Muncaster Castle, dominating the Esk valley for miles around. John Ruskin described it as "Heaven's gate". Open to the public all year round, the castle is a treasure trove of art and antiques; the castle's glorious grounds are home to an unusual owl centre.

▼ **Ennerdale Water**
The most westerly of the lakes, Ennerdale has few visitors even at the height of summer due to its remote location. In the last week of August the Ennerdale Show takes place at the small village of Ennerdale Bridge which lies on the western side of the lake. Ennerdale Water is dominated by the great cliffs of Pillar Fell, on the right of the photograph.